Foreword by Thierry Laplanche

THE 5 SS OF MONEY

OVERCOMING THE
MIDDLE CLASS SQUEEZE

OBSTACLES
PRESS

ESSENTIALS SERIES

First Edition, July 2016
10 9 8 7 6 5 4 3 2 1

Published by:
Obstaclés Press
200 Commonwealth Court
Cary, NC 27511

lifeleadership.com

ISBN 978-0-99712-129-2
Library of Congress Control Number: 2016908268

Cover design and layout by Norm Williams, nwa-inc.com

Printed in the United States of America

*There is at least one fundamental difference
between the 'haves' and
the 'have nots,' and it is
central to the middle class squeeze.*

CONTENTS

Foreword
By Thierry Laplanche

A good understanding, even a mastery of personal finance is indispensable to anyone who is seeking his or her ideal lifestyle. Whether it comes to a hard worker concerned about making ends meet, a student forced to live within a tight budget, a young married couple awaiting their first child, an entrepreneur launching a new company or a philanthropist funding charitable works, the money question is at the forefront of everyone's mind. Yet very few people take the time to educate themselves intentionally and intelligently about the subject. In their concern to take advantage of the immediate gratification advocated by this consumer society, most people finance their lifestyle through debt. As a result, they sacrifice their future and imprison themselves in what my mentor, Orrin Woodward, calls the 'financial matrix'. The disastrous consequences of this poor financial management are to be observed not only at the individual level, but they also extend to the whole community, the entire nation and even to the world. Today, the middle class is becoming steadily poorer and the level of household debt is growing at an alarming rate, while inflation and the cost of living are increasing exponentially.

To escape from this vicious circle, people wrongly believe that the solution lies in increasing the number of hours they work so as to raise their income, or in switching to a more lucrative profession without altering their way of thinking and their financial behavior. They believe that they can treat an illness without having first made the diagnosis and can just stick a Band-Aid on the wound, whereas what it really needs is stitching up. I have always been impressed by the ordered and methodical approach we use in medicine, my first profession. For every clinical case, every patient, four steps have to be followed: gather the facts (patient history), examine the patient, confirm the doctor's clinical impression using laboratory analyses and finally suggest a treatment.

This book follows exactly the same procedure. It gathers the facts and evaluates the alarming financial situation of an impoverished middle class by presenting thought-provoking statistics. It also explores the real reason why the majority of people are prey to financial problems, highlighting a thing that everyone knows but few actually realize.

This book is like a medical scanner that accurately identifies and confirms the source of the financial problems, very often related to a mental mindset. Better still, it suggests a treatment plan, in a simple and ordered way, showing the path to becoming financially fit.

The 5 S's of Money will inspire you, dear reader, to master and apply the few simple things that will enable you to find a way out of your debts, to create surplus income, and to climb the steps of the YOU, Inc. Hierarchy in order to benefit from the opportunities that life has to offer. At a different level, it will prompt you to identify your mission in life and will offer you fresh ways to look at financial incentives.

I also hope that this book will make you understand and take on board your stewardship responsibility with respect to your financial blessings, so that your healthy and fruitful financial management will give glory to God, and inspire others to greatness so as to improve the world in a unique way.

—Thierry Laplanche
March 2016, Delmas, Haiti

"The real voyage of discovery consists not in seeking new lands but seeing with new eyes."
—Marcel Proust

INTRODUCTION

"…concentrate and simplify…"
—Plotonius

From the top…

Let's jump right in. Some people are facing almost overwhelming financial challenges right now. In fact, it's worse than just a temporary downturn in the economy. As a group, the whole middle class is experiencing a downward economic spiral, and it doesn't show signs of ending anytime soon.

Why is this happening? Who caused it? Is it self-inflicted, or is something else going on here? Does it have something to do with the rise of Asia? Or globalization? Or politics? What's really happening? Why can't the middle class seem to get ahead anymore?

These kinds of questions are now daily faire for many people. They arise at the water cooler, while picking up the kids from school, and during lunch breaks. But the even harder questions are often even more important:

What can we do about it?

Is there a solution?

> As a group, the whole middle class is experiencing a downward economic spiral, and it doesn't show signs of ending anytime soon.

Is the collapse of our middle class lifestyles reversible?

If we *can* fix things, is leading the solution up to the government, Wall Street, Silicon Valley, the Federal Reserve, or someone else? Or do we need to make changes ourselves?

How long do we have?

Will our children be caught in this same economic decline?

This book answers these questions, and other important concerns about the current middle class squeeze that is making it harder and harder for good, hard-working people to make ends meet—and actually get ahead financially. Every family needs this information.

Let's Deal With This Head-On!

This book introduces and directly tackles the 5 S's of money:

> These are the 5 S's of money. Understanding and applying them can bring a huge, immediate and lasting improvement to your personal and family finances.

Statistics: What is really happening to the middle class? We need to know these truths that the politicians and government don't want us to know.

Struggles: What can we expect to face financially in the months and years just ahead, and what should we do about it?

Source: What is causing this decline of the middle class? There is a specific, real reason that this is happening, but few people know about it. It is now time for us to understand the true Source of middle class decline and take action to turn things around.

Solutions: How can we reverse the widespread economic decline and turn it into a major opportunity and financial upturn for our families? Learn what really works!

Strategies: What are the specific things we need to know and do to put ourselves and our families on strong financial footing, stop falling behind, and really, truly get ahead in the money game?

These are the 5 S's of money. Understanding and applying them can bring a huge, immediate and lasting improvement to your personal, family and overall finances. Learn them. Use them. Share them with loved ones.

The 5 S's of money can drastically change your future.

*"Our biggest failure
is our failure to see patterns."*
—Marilyn Ferguson

THE FIRST "S" OF MONEY

STATISTICS

"...Statistics [are]...about collecting information and putting it in an order that makes sense."
—Lauren Stamile

"...we have a debt tsunami coming..."
—Paul Ryan

Stats Worth Considering

Despite Mark Twain's famous quip that Statistics are just a higher level of lies, the right kind of Statistics can tell us a lot about money. And about people. In fact, well-considered Statistics can tell us a great deal about a nation, a society, and a generation. They can help us see trends, cycles, and forecast coming challenges or opportunities.

Let's begin this book by learning about twenty key Statistics that paint a very interesting, and sober, picture of today's world, our economy, and what's ahead for the people in our nation. Each of the twenty is worth pondering closely, and together they portray a powerful snapshot of current America and the middle class.

Food Stamps Nation

1. The number of people in the United States receiving "food stamps" (now called the Supplemental Nutrient Assistance Program (SNAP), where the government provides free food to needy individuals and families) rose from 17 million in 1975 to over 47 million by 2013.

> The number of people in the United States receiving "food stamps" rose from 17 million in 1975 to over 47 million by 2013.

This tells us a lot about our nation. With approximately 310 million Americans, this amounts to over 15 percent of the population. This doesn't even include the many others who qualify for food stamps but don't use them, for whatever reason.

In a nation as seemingly prosperous as the United States, this number (47 million on food stamps) is both striking and surprising.

The Shrinking Middle Class

2. Likewise, according to the Center for American Progress, fewer households are now earning enough income to qualify as "middle class." Though many don't want to admit it, they are slipping into the lower classes. In 1970, over 50.3 percent of people in the United States earned enough to qualify for the middle class bracket. This half of the population literally defined what it meant to be the middle part of the economy.

By 2010, in contrast, the number of people earning middle class income was down to 42 percent, and it is still decreasing.[1]

The median household income for the entire nation is $52,000 but for members of the middle class the median is $41,000. Note that this is calculated by household; the actual per person median income is just over $26,000 for the entire nation, and below $21,000 for those in the middle class.

These per person numbers paint a more accurate picture of what most families are experiencing, since not all households have two full-time wage earners.

Also, while in 1970 people in the middle class bracket earned 62 percent of the nation's income, by 2015 they earned just 43 percent.[2] The number of people in the middle class is shrinking, and the standard of living for those in the middle class is decreasing as well.[3]

> The number of people in the middle class is shrinking, and the standard of living for those in the middle class is decreasing as well.

Rising Cost of Living

3. As if the first two trends above aren't bad enough, the prices we pay for things have significantly adjusted, due to inflation, during recent decades. For example, between 1970 and 2009:

- The price of food rose 29%
- The cost of gasoline went up 18%
- Rent and utility costs increased 41%
- Health care prices rose 50%
- The cost of college went up 80% for community colleges, and 113% for a private college/university
- The price of a home went up 97%[4]

These price increases brought inevitable financial losses to a number of American households and families. More and more people have slipped out of the middle class into a need for food assistance and other government or charitable support. Just think of it: A lot of people can't even put food on their table!

> The median family debt went from an average of $25,000 per family in 1989 to over $70,000 per family in 2010. It's getting harder to make ends meet, and harder to stay financially afloat.

This goes far beyond Statistics. This is a serious problem in our nation. In an NBC News/*Esquire* survey 64 percent of respondents said they either don't make enough to pay their bills or just barely make enough.[5] Only 35 percent said they make enough to spend a little on extras.[6]

Skyrocketing Debt

4. Of course, we all need things like food, housing, transportation and health care. Yet according to the Center for American Progress, the median family debt went from an average of $25,000 per family in 1989 to over $70,000 per family in 2010. In Canada, according to the Bank of Montreal's 2015 Annual Debt Report, the average household debt was $92,699. It's getting harder to make ends meet, and harder to stay financially afloat.

People are still working hard, and in many cases both parents are doing their best to pay the bills. Yet most families now turn to debt in an attempt to make ends meet. Not surprisingly, these hard-working families are very concerned about their childrens' economic futures.

Debt that Lasts a Lifetime

5. The average family is now in debt at the level of 154% of their gross annual income! And in Canada, according to debtcanada.ca, by the end of 2014 average household debt was 163% of average disposable income. With interest, this means that most families will still be paying for this debt ten, twenty, and even thirty years from now.

According to the 2010 U.S. Census, the average U.S. household has the following outstanding debts:

Mortgage	$70,323
Student Loan	$11,245
Revolving Credit	$7,630
Vehicle Loan	$8,163[7]
Total	$97,361

ValuePenguin.com shows that by 2014 the average household credit card debt had grown to $9,831, while the age groups with the highest credit card debts are: first, 45-54 years old, and second, those 35-44 years of age. And note this alarming trend: "[T]he average American today holds 52% more [credit card] debt today than they did a decade ago."[8]

Debt has become something many Americans deal with from their teen years, all the way through adulthood, during retirement, and right up to the time of death. For many people, the old quip that the two things you can count on are death and taxes has added a third component: debt.

Retiring Without Resources

6. The Center for Retirement Research reported that 53% of

> "One in three Americans has absolutely no money saved to their name."

American households are now at risk of not having enough money in retirement to maintain their current living standards during their elderly years. And actual retirement ages for most people keep increasing—we're working longer and longer after age 65.

Another report called the new model of retirement by the catchy title: "No Retirement." It warned that, "One in three Americans has absolutely no money saved to their name. In 1983 over 60 percent of American workers had some kind of defined-benefit [retirement] pension plan. Today that number is below 20 percent."[9] According to the Huffington Post, the average Canadian age 55-64 with no pension benefits has just over $3,000 saved for retirement.

Moreover, the number of seniors who are waiting to retire is growing. The number of 75-year-olds who are still working, for example, increased 241 percent between 1980 and 2014.[10]

Dying Broke

> Many Americans aren't just living paycheck to paycheck, they are flat broke.

7. An Ernst and Young study found that 75 percent of North Americans can expect to see all their assets spent before they die. In other words, they'll die as broke

as the day they were born. In truth, most of them will die in debt—financially worse off than when they were born. This is hardly the American Dream most of today's citizens were taught to expect.

No Longterm Savings

8. Indeed, over one third of American workers have less than $1,000 saved for their retirement. This brings to mind the words of Tennessee Williams: "You can be young without money, but you can't be old without it." Even on the high end, sixty percent of workers have less than $25,000 saved for retirement. This isn't going to get them very far.

No Emergency Savings

9. According to a Princeton University/University of Chicago study, forty percent of Americans say they couldn't come up with $2,000 if they needed it. Many people aren't just living paycheck to paycheck, they are flat broke.

The Huge Price of Interest

10. As mentioned, debt is now a serious plague around the nation. It's actually worse than most people realize. For example, the average American spends 34.5 percent of *every* take home dollar on interest. This is big. Imagine what you could do with an additional 34.5 percent of every dollar you make…

But, sadly, for most people, this goes directly to interest on past debt-based purchases.

National Government Debt is Rising

11. In the year 1980, the gross debt of the United States government was 42 percent of our GDP—not a good ratio. [11] But by 2012 U.S. debt reached 107 percent of our annual GDP![12] This is unsustainable, and the national debt is now over $19 trillion! Note that it was just above $10 trillion dollars in January of 2009—it is rising very quickly.

To put this in perspective, today, whatever else an American owes (or doesn't owe), every man, woman and child owes more than $55,000 for the national debt. To figure out how much you own, multiply $55,000 by the number of people in your family.

> The average American spends 34.5 percent of *every* take home dollar on interest.

Although not every man, woman and child will end up paying their share directly, this amount influences credit ratings, loans, lending rates, interest rates, wages, and the costs of goods— thus everyone's finances are indirectly or directly influenced by the debt. When the full amount of national, state, local and unfunded liabilities are added, along with over $40 trillion of private debt, the national debt amount is at least $128 trillion, plus interest.[13]

That's more than eight times the national GDP.[14] And it is rising. This amounts to over $413,000 for every American adult and child.

Poverty Rate Increasing

12. At the same time, the poverty rate in the United States is 4 percent *higher* than it was forty years ago.[15] Still, the top .1 percent of earners are making more than ever, and the .01 percent are making even more.

Specifically, the top .1 percent has increased its prosperity from owning 9 percent of the nation's wealth thirty years ago to 22 percent in 2011.[16] Likewise, by 2011 the top 1 percent of households (those making over $389,000 a year) owned 40% of "the nation's entire wealth."[17]

Many people realize that this is happening, even if they don't know the specific numbers. In one NBC News/*Esquire* survey, 74 percent of respondents said they believe the gap between the very wealthy and everyone else is widening,[18] and 78 percent of them "think elected officials generally enact policies that favor the interests of the wealthy" more than the needs of "all Americans."[19]

People are Working Longer Hours

13. In 1960 the average workweek for full-time employees was around 40 hours (40.24 to be precise),[20] creating an expectation of a 9-5 workday. This lifestyle expectation is still around, but people are actually working much longer hours. According to Gallup, the average workweek for full-time employees is now 47 hours, almost a full workday more than the 40-hour expectation.

Beyond this, forty percent of full-time workers put in 50 hours or more a week, while only 8 percent work less than 40 hours weekly. One in five American workers log more than 60 hours per week.

In short, Americans with full-time jobs are working longer. According to the *Washington Post*, those on salary work even more: 49 hours on average for salaried workers, and over half of workers on salary put in 50 or more hours weekly.

Unemployment and Underemployment Rates Remain High

14. The real unemployment rate (which includes those who are out of work and are actively looking for a job, those who are out of work and have stopped looking for work, and those who are *underemployed*) remains above 10 percent. This means that literally a tenth (or more) of our nation isn't productively employed. This is a great economic problem for the country, and especially for those who don't have a job but need one.

> Today's "average two-income...families have less discretionary income—and less money to put away for a rainy day—than the single-income family of a generation ago."

One of the main reasons for high real unemployment is that health care costs continue to skyrocket, leaving employers and companies who want to increase their number of employees unable to hire.

More Bankruptcies

15. The number of U.S. bankruptcies went up approximately thirty percent between 2006 and 2014, according to the Administrative Office of the U.S. Courts. This includes both business and non-business bankruptcies. In fact, they went up from roughly 300,000 bankruptcies in 1980 to over 900,000 in 2014.[21]

Less Discretionary Money

16. As an article in *Today* put it: "The average two-income family earns far more today than did the single-breadwinner family of a generation ago. And yet, once they have paid the mortgage, the car payments, the taxes, the health insurance, and the day-care bills, today's dual-income families have

> The number of U.S. bankruptcies went up approximately thirty percent between 2006 and 2014.

less discretionary income—and less money to put away for a rainy day—than the single-income family of a generation ago."

The report continues, "A generation ago, a single breadwinner who worked diligently and spent carefully could assure his family a comfortable position in the middle class. But the frenzied bidding wars [mainly for homes in high-result school districts, and costs of college], fueled by families with two incomes, changes the game for single-income families as well, pushing them down the economic ladder...."

"Married parents are in trouble because they have spent every last penny and then some just to buy a middle-class life for their children....The Two-Income Trap is thick with irony. Middle-class mothers went into the workforce in a calculated effort to give their families an economic edge. Instead, millions of them are now in the workplace just so their families can break even.... Today's middle-class mother is trapped: She can't afford to work, and she can't afford to quit."[22]

The Conference Board Consumer Research Center reported that households that earn less than $50,000 annually make up almost 60 percent of households but only have about 3% of the nation's discretionary income. In other words, when the bills are paid, on average they have almost nothing left, less than $159 per month.[23]

Note that the poor (households that make less than $20,000 per year), have less than $31 per month of discretionary money.[24]

Homes Cost A Lot More

17. Traditionally, a key part of the American Dream was for every family to own its own home. Yet the costs of home owner-ship have drastically increased in recent decades. And the word "drastic" here may actually be an understatement.

The numbers speak for themselves. According to the U.S. Census, the median cost of a home (including lot/land) by year continues to skyrocket:

1965	$20,000
1970	$23,400
1975	$39,300
1980	$64,600
1985	$84,300
1990	$122,900
1995	$133,900
2000	$169,000
2010	$221,800
2015	$305,000

In major cities, the price of housing is even higher. In New York City, for example, the average home price is more than 10 times average annual income.[25] San Francisco is 8.8 times annual income and Los Angeles is at 7.5, while Vancouver is at 9.7 and Toronto at 9.2 times annual income.[26]

Many people are paying more for housing than they can afford, while many younger people and others in the middle class are avoiding home ownership altogether. In fact, renting is a smart financial decision for many people in this economy.

Unfortunately, even renting is a challenge for many people. As one report put it: "Today, most poor renting families spend more than half of their income on housing, and eviction has become commonplace…"[27] Those who do get evicted are often permanently shifted into a life of poverty in the lower class.[28]

"Three Generation" Households on the Rise

18. In 1980 just 12% of the U.S. population lived in a multi-generational household with children, adults, and elderly relatives.[29] By 2008, this number was up to 16% of the population, which according to Pew Research Center "represents a significant trend reversal."[30] The elderly moved in with adult children (or vice versa) in numbers not seen for three decades—59 percent of individuals living in multi-generational homes in 2008 were 65 or older.[31]

> The number of U.S. bankruptcies went up approximately thirty percent between 2006 and 2014.

In 58 percent of these situations the adults and their families moved in with the elderly relative, while in 42 percent of the cases an elderly relative moved in with their adult children and family.[32] A major part of this change was economic challenges, financial strain, and increasing costs brought on by a struggling economy—in the Great Recession and since.

In fact, the number of multi-generational households drastically increased between 2007 and 2009, when the Great Recession began.[33] Financial woes and a sluggish economy have driven this trend.

> The middle class is under significant and growing financial pressure.

Even "Four Generation" Households are Growing in Number

19. The younger generation is also facing an economic crisis that few people know about. Or, at least, not many Americans realize the extent of this problem. Twenty-somethings and even thirty-somethings are moving back home to live with Mom and Dad in large numbers. In 1980 54% of 18-24 year old men lived with their parents, while by 2010 that number had risen to 57%.[34] In 1980 43% of 18-24 year old women lived with their parents, compared with 49% by 2010.[35]

But, driven by a bad economy, the biggest homeward trend is among 25-34 year olds. While 11% of men and 7% of women in this age group lived with their parents in 1980, by 2010 the number was 16% of men and 11% of women.[36] Often these older adult children bring spouses and children with them.

One of the main reasons for this trend is that while in 1991 the overall cost of a college experience was almost the same as the earnings of new college graduates, today the costs are drastically higher than the income.[37] The gap is being addressed by living at home and having many expenses covered by older parents.

Approximately 25 million American adults now "live at home with parents because they're unemployed or underemployed."[38] The results are devastating for some people. For example, the median net worth of U.S. adults 35

A number of businesses now hire new employees at 25 percent less than they did before the Great Recession.

and younger was $11,621 in 1984.[39] By 2009 it was $3,662,[40] roughly a two-thirds decline.

The Great Recession of 2008-2011 Really Hurt

20. Most people don't realize just how bad the Great Recession was, or how hard it hit the middle class. Between 2006 and 2011, property prices decreased by 33% on the whole.[41] Even worse, many investors saw their portfolios lose half their value.[42] That's half!

After years of investing, this was a major shock. And a number of businesses now hire new employees at 25 percent less than they did before the Great Recession.[43] Its impact was real and lasting, especially to the middle class.

Summary

So...that's enough Statistics for now. When you read a list like these twenty stats, it's easy to start feeling a bit numb after a while. You know the next number is coming, and that it's going to be shocking. You hope it doesn't describe you, and then about halfway into it you realize that it kind of does...

We could go on with more Statistics, but the ones we've already mentioned suffice to make something very, very clear:

**The middle class is under significant
and growing financial pressure.**

The Statistics of the current economy show a consistent and serious pattern of economic problems, financial decline, and difficulty for most American workers and their families. This is very important, to all of us.

In short, the first "S" of money—Statistics—plainly shows that for many people today finances are a major, pressing concern. This will likely only increase if world and national economic challenges continue and increase in the years ahead.

"Choose always the way that seems right; however rough it may be."
—Pythagoras

THE SECOND "S" OF MONEY

STRUGGLE

"This...is addressed to the young—in years or in spirit—who are not afraid to know and are not ready to give up."
—Ayn Rand

"Never, never, never give up."
—Winston Churchill

Have You Ever Faced Financial Problems?

Money and finances can be a serious Struggle. Almost everyone has—or has had—money challenges at some point in his or her life. The question about such challenges, and all challenges for that matter, isn't whether you've had them or not, but how you handle them when they come.

Most importantly: What are the predictable, universal financial problems that come to almost everyone? Knowing about them can help you prepare, and knowing that they are normal and widespread can help you relax and face them effectively when they arise.

In this chapter we'll learn about 10 financial challenges that almost everyone eventually faces. Half of these—what we'll call "The Big 5"—are closely connected, meaning that they combine together to increase the Struggle for lasting financial fitness. The other five are more individual, and some of them are actually even bigger for most people than the "Big 5," but all of them can be a challenge.

For many people, taxes are the biggest single expense over a lifetime.

Together these 10 foreseeable financial issues make up the bulk of almost everyone's money Struggles. They are a common experience for pretty much anyone who handles money. In fact, these Struggles are in many ways the culprits causing the Statistics we discussed in the last chapter. Let's learn what they are.

Taxes

#1: TAXES. Taxes can be a major financial Struggle. Anticipating them, saving for them, strategizing about them, making sure to be honest and also wise and frugal—it all adds up to a lot of work.

For almost everyone, taxes are their single biggest expense over a lifetime. Thus it is wise to be careful about taxes and don't overpay. That said, we don't recommend that you dig in deep and find the "hard rugged edge" of ways to pay as little tax as possible. It's not a place to mess around or get cute. If you avoid getting creative on taxes, and instead pay what you owe, you'll probably never have a tax problem (of the kind where your governments put you through the audit process, charge late fees and interest, and the like).

In short, don't get cute on your taxes, or cheat in any way—or push the envelope. Know what you can write off, and do it. But don't push it beyond the norm. This is one area in which you are well advised to hire a professional.

As mentioned, taxes will be one of life's biggest expenses, and that's working against your financial fitness. That's why taxes are part of the Struggle.

When Your Money Is Gradually Worth Less and Less

#2: INFLATION. The next Struggle is called inflation. This is an increase in the money supply that forces prices to go up. Note that it doesn't increase or push up the *value* of the items you buy, just their price. So you get to pay more money for the same item, of the same value, just because there is more money in circulation.

Here's how this works. Let's say you are reading this book at your local bookstore, and while you're there the bookstore announces that they're holding a rare book auction in 2 minutes. You walk over to see what they're selling, and you find out that they're auctioning off signed copies of your favorite author's top five books.

The only catch is that you have to pay in cash. So you pull out your wallet and realize that you only have $21 on hand. Hopefully, you tell yourself, this will be enough to get one of the books.

You see other people looking at their cash, and you can tell everyone is basically in the same boat. They have debit cards and credit cards, but who carries around a lot of cash these days?

You hear people lamenting that they only have $14.50 or a ten dollar bill, and you get excited. Maybe you'll win one of these books after all.

Now, imagine that something amazing happens. While the auctioneer is explaining how great the first book is, and unbeknownst to you, someone sneaks in the back of the room and starts passing out $100 bills to the crowd. Guess what will happen?

That's right. Inflation. Suddenly the average bid on the books will go up a lot. Just the addition of extra cash to the room will drive up the price. Because of the increase in the money supply, the bids on the books will greatly increase.

> **The amount of available cash in an economy increases the amounts of money people are willing to spend on things. That's inflation.**

The amount of available cash in an economy increases the amounts of money people are willing to spend on things. That's inflation. Increase the amount of money in the room, and you likely increase the price of things purchased in the room. The same thing happens in a larger economy, like a nation or even a global market.

Note that inflation can happen in a couple of ways. First, because we live under a fiat currency system (meaning that the government currency has value mainly because the government has dictated that people must accept it), the government (usually through their central bank, or the Federal Reserve in the U.S.) can increase inflation simply by printing more money or digitally increasing the money supply.

When this happens, each individual dollar buys less. The more currency the government puts into circulation, the higher prices rise. In fact, if you already have money before the government inflates it by printing more, the money you already hold will suddenly be worth less—and buy less.

Second, inflation can be caused by a Fractional Reserve Banking system, which occurs when the banks loan out more money than they actually take in on deposit. This causes the effective supply of money to increase, and prices naturally rise as a result.

All of this is bad for your finances, because your money won't buy as much as it used to. It's worth less. (In some extreme cases in history, inflation got so bad that the money went from "worth less" to entirely "worthless".)

Of course, as mentioned, inflation isn't good for your spending power. It's part of almost everyone's financial Struggle. And as long as we have a fiat government currency and fractional reserve banking, it's going to be a continual problem (unless deflation occurs, which is beyond the scope of this book but could, in different ways, be even worse).

So, to summarize so far, we're running up against taxes in our finances, and we're also running against what's often called "The Invisible Tax," called inflation.

We are surrounded by and bombarded with materialistic messages.

Together these take a serious cut out of every dollar we earn.

"The Big 5"

Next we'll learn about the "Big 5" financial Struggles that often combine into one *major* challenge. Here's how this works:

- It starts with #3: MATERIALISM.

Our culture is inundated with materialistic messaging. From the commercials on television to the ads that pop up online, to the billboards we see as we drive and the conversations people around us have about the new ads they've seen and the new things they want to buy—we are surrounded by and bombarded with materialistic messages.

We are sold on a number of things that are "truthy" but not truth. They sound all right, and we kind of buy into them, but upon further inspection they're built on falsehoods. For example:

- "If you can afford the payments, you can afford the purchase."
- "Everybody's doing it—that's just how it works."
- "If you don't buy things on credit, you'll never have anything nice."
- "You really need this. Your spouse (or kids) deserves it."
- "You need to get into debt so you can build up your credit."
- "Everybody uses student loans to get through school. You'll pay them back easily once your degree gets you a great job."
- "If you buy the newer, more expensive car, you can get a better rate on your loan."
- "It's just normal to have a thirty-year mortgage."

These phrases are more filled with falsehoods than truths. They're akin to saying: "You should smoke a little crack, so if you ever end up smoking more it won't kill you."

Huh?

Ridiculous.

These kinds of falsehoods often sound good to the unsuspecting person, but they're not real. They don't stand up to truth in the actual financial world.

They are really just false dogmas of the philosophy of Materialism. And materialism is all around us, day and night, at home and at work.

As bestselling authors Neil Postman and Steve Powers put it:

- "The backbone, the heart, the soul, the fuel, the DNA (choose whatever metaphor you wish) of… television in America is the commercial. This is as true of the television news shows as it is any other form of programming….

- "With so much money being spent…for airtime, advertisers…want their messages to be effective. To make sure that happens, they bring in a small army of specialists, people who are experts in making commercials.

- "Over months of work, artists, statisticians, writers, psychologists, researchers, musicians, cinematographers, lighting consultants, camera operators, producers, directors, set builders, composers, models, actors, audio experts, executives, and technicians will toil for one single objective: to make a commercial that will make you buy a product or idea. Time and talent costs can be $500,000 for a short commercial."[44]

The phrase "make you" in this sentence is significant. Commercial makers put so much money into marketing and making these ads because they want you to buy. Not just to think the product or actor is cool. They want you to buy. They do whatever they can to "make you" buy.

Such marketing directly increases our society's Materialism. And there is a lot of it. Every day new ads come online, and others air on television.

Commercials tap directly into our emotions, trying to convince us to buy things we probably wouldn't otherwise. For example:

> We are seldom told to be frugal, wait until we have the cash to buy a car or home, or never buy anything with credit unless we have the money already.

- "Boredom, anxiety, rejection, fear, envy, sloth—in TV commercials there are remedies for each of these, and more. The remedies are called Scope, Comet, Toyota, Bufferin, Alka-Seltzer, and Budweiser....A commercial for Alka-Seltzer, for example, does not teach you to avoid overeating. Gluttony is perfectly acceptable—maybe even desirable.

- "The point of the commercial is that your gluttony is no problem. Alka-Seltzer will handle it...."[45]

- These kinds of ads aren't just on television, they're all around us. Materialism is promoted day after day, and eventually many people fall for it. When they do, they buy things—often more than they need, and frequently a lot more than they can afford.

- And materialism isn't just about "fixing" your problems. It also emphasizes things you want, stuff you just crave or desire to own. Materialism tries to convince you to buy more and more and more.

- Materialism leads to #4: DEBT.

Along with all this materialism, we are told to buy this and buy that, and we are assured that the more expensive items are available through financing. Credit card offers come in the mail, promising loyalty points, lower rates, and lists of special benefits. Banks compete for our business. Many stores, hotels, airlines, and other businesses offer their own credit cards or other financing programs.

Even many of our kids' schools encourage programs that give the school points and rewards every time we buy from a certain store or use a certain credit card. Charities and some churches do the same.

We are seldom—except by wise parents, mentors, or leaders—told to be frugal, wait until we have the cash to buy a car or home, or never buy anything with credit unless we have the money already. Society consistently tells us the opposite: "Buy what you want, put it on credit, and then buy even more of whatever you want."

This leads to debt. And debt is a very big Struggle indeed. Once in debt, it can take years or decades to climb out of the hole. For some people, it is the most difficult financial Struggle of all. For anyone who gets into serious debt, it a serious challenge.

As mentioned before, the average American uses 34.5 percent of his or here take home pay just to pay the *interest* on past debts! Just the interest!

One of the biggest ways young people get pulled into a debt lifestyle is through student loans. So many voices— including the school administration and the government— tell students that loans will be a great help to them. And as soon as they apply for the loan, they find that a number of additional credit card offers come in the mail.

They talk to their friends and roommates and find that "everybody's doing it," and loans become a part of their everyday life. Then, when they wonder if they would like better transportation, they automatically consider a car loan. It snowballs from one loan to the next.

Many people spend their whole life working to pay off loans—and getting more loans along the way. Then they co-sign to help their young-adult children do the same, and the cycle deepens and repeats.

In fact, many people find that student loans can't even be forgiven through bankruptcy, and they're still paying for them many years after they leave college. But perhaps the worst legacy of student loans is that young people are saddled very early in life with a habit of using debt to meet their financial needs.

- Debt leads to # 5: INTEREST.

Of course, when you are in debt, you don't just have to pay back what you borrowed. You also owe interest on everything you buy with credit.

Interest is a major Struggle. Einstein quipped that compound interest is the eighth wonder of the world, because of its ability to grow over time.

Many people spend their whole life working to pay off loans—and getting more loans along the way.

When you get this power of compounding working *against* you, you're in trouble. You know how it works. Look at how much you'd pay for a home if you bought it without a loan, then add up what all the monthly payments over the course of the loan actually amount to, and you realize that a mortgage means you'll typically pay between two and three times the original purchase price!

In a world where the average home costs over $305,000, that means you could pay more than $700,000 through compound interest. In fact, the word "compounding" even sounds a bit violent! "It's compounding, oh no!" Just when you got hit once, it's coming around next month to pound you again!

In fact, people get caught in a spiral of materialistic debt because when interest rates dip they refinance their mortgage and start the thirty-year compounding all over again! The amounts people pay due to compound interest are staggering.

The mortgage industry lives on this, and typically promotes "easy" mortgages with slogans and ad campaigns like: "Push Button Get Mortgage", and "No Branches=Great Rates".[46]

Over time, perhaps the biggest problem with interest is what happens next, in items # 6 and 7 below:

- Interest leads to #6: Becoming someone else's ASSET.

  When you owe money, you automatically become someone else's asset. You work to pay them. You are an income source for them, struggling and working to benefit your creditors.

  They won't let you stop paying them—after all, you're their asset. They expect you to keep making them money. If you make choices that hurt the flow of money from your work to their accounts, they'll take steps to stop you. You owe them. And they'll collect.

  This means that you truly are, to a certain extent, a kind of debt-slave to whomever you owe. This keeps a lot of people from getting ahead, making needed changes, or improving things in their lives. They feel stuck for good reason: because they are.

- And finally, being someone else's asset leads to #7: Becoming your own LIABILITY.

  Your past choices about debt can really get in the way of what you want right now. Your past choices to use credit can block what is best for you now, and what you need to do.

  When those past choices are a major Liability for you, you're stuck. You'll have to pass on great opportunities, give up things that would have been a great blessing to you and your loved ones, and in other ways miss out. When you are a liability to yourself, because of past debt choices, you keep yourself from living the life you truly want and dream about.

But the only way to overcome this is to stop being your own Liability, meaning that you've got to stop being the bank's Asset. You have to pay off your debts and become debt-free.

Debt freedom is true freedom. Without debt freedom, you're always someone's Asset and your own Liability.

These 5 things combined (Materialism, Debt, Interest, Being Somebody's Asset, and Being Your Own Liability) create quite a cycle. They are a big deal, and hard to overcome.

But the most amazing thing about these 5 combined financial Struggles is that most people spend a lot of their life repeating and reliving all 5, over and over. Materialism® Debt® Interest® Being Somebody's Asset ® Being Your Own Liability. The cycle can be endless, if you let it.

People do it repeatedly. And it sucks much of the happiness out of many lives.

Don't get caught in the cycle of these 5 financial Struggles. Avoid them like the plague. When you see Materialism and Debt temptations coming, run the other way. As fast as you can!

Teach your children, partners and friends to do the same. The Materialism® Being Your Own Liability cycle is a life killer. It kills your dreams, dries up your goals, and can shut down your happiness. Avoid it.

> **The good news is that you don't have to know everything all at once.**

Getting Help is Hard to Do

#8: HIGH-PRICED "PROFESSIONALS."

The next Struggle is wasting money on high-priced financial professionals. Here's how this happens: Many times people feel that finances are complex, and difficult, so they hire financial "professionals" to help them manage their money and make better financial decisions. Sadly, this can frequently be a waste of money because many so-called financial advisors are just salesmen in disguise. Or, the professionals may be well intended and well trained, but they'll never handle your money as well as you—if you get the training and financial understanding yourself.

In fact, if you do need the financial advice of a professional, it is usually best to hire him or her by the hour or the task to answer your questions and teach you what you need to learn (such as a tax professional we referred to earlier). Then you can do what the professional taught you, or at least limit their involvement to one area of expertise (such as doing your taxes). Many professionals aren't paid based on how well they take care of your money, but rather on what they can sell you. It is often better to just pay up front for solid financial advice without it being tied to commissions and sales.

This can be part of the Struggle, until you learn how to do a lot of things yourself, or to hire only solid advice. Again, learn how to manage your money yourself—as much as possible.

"But It's Complicated!"

#9: COMPLICATION.

Another money Struggle is that it can all feel so complicated. So frustrating, complex, and even overwhelming. There are so many financial words, phrases and terms—what do they all mean? How are you supposed to learn them? What do you need to know first?

This can feel frustrating. You're listening to or reading about sophisticated things like "collateralized" or "swaps" or "getting things rated" or...

Take a deep breath. If you know these terms, no problem. If not, relax. The truth is that many financial products have been put together by financial experts and geniuses and people with long experience in the financial field. There are people who are financially talented, or creative, just like in any other career or field. But the good news is that you don't have to know everything all at once. You just need to know what you need to know right now.

Remember that finance is a field or economic sector, like medicine, law, or engineering. And just like these other fields, the experts like to use technical terms to keep you hiring them for their expertise. Part of the confusion and complication is by design. The professionals want you to need them. Otherwise they won't get paid.

The truth is that a lot of things about finances *are* complicated. But when you need help with complicated things, you'll be able to find experts (to teach you what you need to know, not to take over your finances for you).

Money stress is constant for many people, and even for others it can mess with our emotions.

For most people, however, for the regular Joe's and Jane's in the world, finances aren't that complicated. In fact, they won't become complicated until you've learned how to do the basic, simple things really well.

What does this mean? It means that for the most part only the people who do a few very simple, very basic things with money (like build up lots of savings) will ever have enough money to worry about the complicated parts of finance.

The complications of the financial world can add to each person's financial Struggle, to be sure. But don't worry about them. You'll have time to learn about them (after all, that's what this book is all about)! And if you ever really need to know about the complicated and sophisticated areas of finance, it will probably mean that you've built up enough money in your accounts that you can afford some expert advice.

The real key is to learn how to do the few simple things that will bring you a bunch of extra cash in your accounts—and then *do* them. The good news is that these things are *not complicated*! (We'll learn what they are in later chapters.)

Time for a Melt Down?

#10: STRESS.

All of the 9 Struggles outlined above, including the complication of financial terms, phrases, and expectations, can work together to make finances seem stressful. Yet, as with so many things, the Struggle is worth the journey. Learning to really understand and master your finances will bring so many blessings and opportunities into your life.

But money stress is constant for many people, and even for others it can mess with their emotions. Indeed, money has emotions attached to it. Concerns and worries about money are usually not very fun or enjoyable. Debt can be especially stressful, and debt payment deadlines can feel even worse.

The feelings of lack, want and need are stressful, and can even cause long-term anxiety. Money stresses can cloud our judgment, and inhibit our ability to think clearly about options, Solutions and choices.

Together the stress, complications and other Struggles of money can be difficult. That's why we're learning about them here, so you'll know what to expect, and most importantly, what to do about them..

Again, the Solutions are few and basic. We'll learn about them very soon. But right now it's helpful to remember this: The Solutions *are* few and basic. You can do them. And when you do, your finances will fall into place and you'll have a lot more control over your money.

Summary

All ten of these Struggles can be overcome if you know what to do, and if you take the right actions and do the right things. But first you have to know the right Solutions, and then you have to know how to effectively implement them. As we said above, this is actually quite simple.

So far we've talked about twenty significant Statistics of money, and ten very typical and even universal Struggles of money. In covering these first two S's of money, we have outlined the problem.

Next we're going to turn to the Source of the problem. Most people don't understand what it is (not *really*), so they have no idea how to solve it effectively. But when you *do* understand the actual source of most money problems, you'll have the power to drastically improve your finances.

So, what *is* the Source of most money problems?

It's not what you think. Most people have no idea...

*"Do the thing
and you shall have the power."*
—Emerson

THE THIRD "S" OF MONEY

SOURCE

"[A] small thing may give analogy of great things..."
—Lucretius

*"Risk-taking, and the freedom to pursue huge risks,
is America's most important asset."*
—Nassim Taleb

**Almost Everyone Knows This,
But Few Actually *Realize* It**

The Source of most money problems is that people think the key to money is to work for it. But this viewpoint about money is only partly true. The rest of the formula is lost on most people. And this causes numerous financial problems.

In fact, our whole society is caught in this trap. Bestselling author Alvin Toffler taught in his book *The Third Wave* that modern society was organized on six basic principles.[47] These six guidelines dominate almost all the major institutions in our advanced nations—education, banking, government, business, and finance, among others.[48]

The six organizing principles of the modern world are:

- Standardization
- Specialization
- Synchronization
- Concentration
- Maximization
- Centralization[49]

Moreover, Toffler argued, we can understand the world very well simply by looking at how any major institution in society applies these six goals. This is incredibly relevant to how each person earns, keeps, gives, spends and manages money. Indeed, the modern system is largely designed to benefit those who help the system.

The many consequences of this way of structuring society is very important to the issue of finances. Here's how:

The divide between those who see people as pawns of big government and big business on the one hand, versus those who see people as free, capable, creative individuals on the other, greatly influences finances.

Most people in modern society are taught to believe in and follow an incorrect and inferior path of personal success, happiness, and making a living—one that benefits the standardized, maximized, centralized system and those who run it, but which hurts the finances of most individuals.

This is a bold statement, but it is true. In more down-to-earth words: A lot of people are beginning to wonder if the financial system is rigged—benefitting those at the top rather than the rest of us.

Moreover, this same incorrect and inferior path is a key Source of most money Struggles for most people. It is the main cause of the middle class squeeze.

The good news is that those who know the Source can get off the wrong path and watch their finances drastically improve. The bad news is that many people have been convinced since childhood that the inferior path is the *only* path. They are reluctant to change, even when it is good for them.

Power Pyramids

As Toffler put it, through history every nation has been run by "The Power Pyramids....Every industry and branch of government soon gave birth to its own establishment, its own powerful 'They.'

"Sports...religion...education...each had its own pyramid of power. A science establishment, a defense establishment, a cultural establishment sprang up."[50] So did a financial establishment of "elites" and even "super-elites."[51] Orrin Woodward calls this establishment a "financial matrix." Speaking of it, he said: "It's that simple. Follow the money. The power elites want money that makes them rich with the least work, and increases their power over others. And they're willing to pay and reward intellectuals and government officials who will help them."

How does this influence the regular person, the Joe's and Jane's in our neighborhoods, communities, church groups and workplaces? The establishment system was designed for the masses to work for the wealthy and big institutions (both corporate and governmental). Almost everyone knows this, but few people fully *realize* what it actually means for most of us.

The Cause

Specifically: The Source of the money Struggles and Statistics outlined above, the greatest Source of the decline of the middle class lifestyle and the American Dream is, in fact, an incorrect view of money. Most elites teach a correct view of money to their children, while the rest of the people typically believe an incorrect view.

If you are caught in this incorrect view of money, your money Struggles will likely continue. If you become aware of the incorrect view, however, and both adopt and apply a *correct* view of money, things can drastically improve for your finances.

> The Source of the money Struggles and Statistics outlined above, the greatest Source of the decline of the middle class, in fact, is an incorrect view of money.

It really is this simple. Most of us were raised with an incorrect "money view." We were taught a flawed perspective of money, and this is the Source of most financial problems for the vast majority of people.

Turning the Crank

To be specific, many of us were taught the wrong view of money as children and young adults, and we were raised to believe that the goal is to make as much money as we can, so we can spend it on what we want.

At this point, someone might ask: "But isn't that true? We know we should avoid debt. But otherwise money is there for us to spend on what we want, right?"

The answer is "no."

This blunt response will probably surprise a lot of people. The truth is that this mindset—make as much as possible so you can spend it as you desire—is a major problem. It is an incorrect view.

> **Money has a lot more uses than to be spent on our wants and needs.**

Money has a lot more uses than to be spent on our wants and needs. It has a lot more uses than merely for us to exchange it when we want things. And knowing this makes a huge difference.

If we start with the wrong idea that money exists so we can buy the things we want, we're probably never going to really understand money—or handle it well—unless we change this mindset. This might seem like a little thing, but it isn't. It's huge.

Most of us were taught to go to school, get good grades to the best of our ability, and then get the best job we can—all so we can turn a Crank. This means that we spend much our young life becoming qualified to turn a Crank, in either employment or business ownership. Then, once we're qualified, we start turning the Crank, and trying to get promoted to higher and more lucrative levels of Crank turning.

The "Crank" is the thing that brings us our income. It might be a job, a career, or a business we build. But whatever it is, we think that income is supposed to come to us

> **We think that if we could only turn the Crank a little harder, or a bit faster, we could make more money.**

from our work, and then be used to buy us stuff. Almost everyone thinks this. "Turn the crank so we can buy some stuff." Wrong!

It's False

It just isn't true. Still, since this is what we believe, we think that if we could only turn the Crank a little harder, or a bit faster, we could make more money. Then, once we're Cranking harder and faster and making a little more, we start to think that if only we could Crank even better or for longer hours, things would improve for us. This cycle causes a lifetime of seeking more money from the Crank, so we can spend more on things we need and want.

Indeed, most people are constantly wishing they had more leverage on the Crank so they could get more income and purchase more stuff. In fact, since they can't afford all the stuff they want, they use debt to make up the difference. Then they have to pay interest on that debt—as we've already discussed—and they soon find that the more debt they have, the less money they have even though they're Cranking harder and faster than ever.

The result? When we talk about getting out of debt, it doesn't sound very fun. *Being* out of debt sounds great, but *getting* there feels like a lot of extra work at the Crank. Not fun at all.

A lot of people think: "Won't we have to drink tap water and eat pork and beans, and ramen, in order to tighten our belts and get out of debt?" Others worry: "Whenever we try to live within our means, we all start being *mean*."

People with this mindset tend to believe that if they got out of debt, the consequence would be wonderful: they'd have more money from the Crank to spend on stuff they want. Even though this kind of thinking got them in trouble in the first place, it's still the way they view things.

In fact, some of you may be wondering what we're even talking about right now. After all, we're saying that the flawed view, the incorrect view of money, is that you should get the best Crank you can, work hard at it to get as much income as you can, and then spend the money on things you want.

"Isn't that what everyone does?" you might be asking. "Isn't that obvious? What other way is there?"

If this is how you were raised or learned to view money, you may be caught in the Second S of Money: the Struggle. This way of viewing money is an almost sure recipe for remaining stuck in the middle class squeeze and facing ongoing money Struggles for the rest of your life. It's a flawed view, and a wrong one.

And, yes, there is a different way to view money. In fact, getting your moneyview right can make all the difference to your financial life.

Now just to be clear, the other way of viewing money is *not* that the government should just give you what you need. That's an even worse moneyview than the Crank approach.

> **Your Crank (job, career, business, etc.) brings you income, but not just to spend.**

So what is the right, more accurate, view of money?

Well, first of all, the problem is not the Crank. It's the whole view of money based on getting the training to get a good job, then getting the best one you can, turning the

Crank as hard as you can day after day, and using the money you earn from the Crank to buy the stuff you want. That's the problem. The whole model is flawed.

We'll learn about the right, correct, view of money in the next chapter. But first, it's crucial to ask yourself a very important question—and make a vitally important decision.

Your Huge, Vital Decision

This decision is going to make all the difference in your life. If you choose the wrong path, your financial Struggles could cling to you forever. If you select the right path, you can be headed for increased financial fitness and more success. It really can be that simple.

Bestselling author Carol Dweck wrote in her book *Mindset* that there are two main types of people. She also taught that all of us get to choose which type we want to be. We might be born with tendencies toward one or the other, but many, many people have chosen to change their focus and become the other type.

These two "types" are a little bit like the Type A and Type B labels nurses sometimes use when working with recovering heart patients. Many of these patients have already experienced heart attacks, and they need to change their lifestyles in order to avoid further heart problems.

Nurses use "Type B" to describe patients who are humble, try hard to do what the doctors and nurses suggest, and relax, sit back and accept that they're in a new reality and need to change their lives in order to recuperate. They eat the new way the doctors prescribe, always take their medication, don't hurry back to the office, and in general do what the health professionals recommend.

> The Solution to money challenges and a wrong view of money begins by learning about money.

"Type A" patients are a different story. They fight every suggestion. They can't wait to go back to eating like they used to, they won't stay in bed and rest as prescribed, they quit taking their medications as soon as they can get away with it, and they start working again months before the doctors give them the okay. In short, they're bad patients, and they often end up right back in the hospital with even worse health problems.

Dweck's two types of people are similar, but slightly different. Instead of Type A versus Type B, Dweck divides healthy, regular people into Type F and Type G. All of us get to choose which type we'll apply in our daily lives.

Type F

Type F people, Dweck taught, have a Fixed mindset. When they learn something new, they typically say something like, "I just can't make that change. I was born this way. This is just how I am. I'm just not good at that." When they hear of a problem, they respond: "That's bad. It's over. Why me?"

Where money is concerned, Type F people learn about the need to put aside the old Crank mentality of money and do something that really works, and they respond with phrases like:

"I'm too old to change."

"That's too hard."

"I grew up learning the other way, and I'm not likely to change now."

"You can't teach on old dog new tricks."

"You pour new wine into old bottles."

"I wish I could improve in this, but my grandparents were in debt, my parents were in debt, and I've been in debt my whole life. That's just the way things are. That's how our family is."

This is the Source of many money Struggles—the limited belief that money is all about using the Crank to earn it and then spending it up, and using debt when the Crank falls short. People who believe this, and refuse to see past it, can stay stuck in the rut of financial problems for a very long time.

Type G

The Type G person, in contrast, has a Growing mindset. When problems or changes come, they respond by saying things such as: "How can we turn this into an opportunity? What an exciting challenge this is! I can't wait to turn this around. This certainly looks like a problem, but I bet we can use it to make things even better than before! Let's use this to go to a whole new level!"

Type G people choose to turn lemons into lemonade, as the old proverb recommends. When Type G people learn about the Third S of Money, the Struggles that come from the false beliefs of earning from the Crank and spending what you earn, they perk up and say things like:

"This is so exciting. I had no idea there was another way. Please tell me what it is…fast!"

"You're blowing my mind. If the Crank view is inaccurate and wrong, what could the right view possibly be? Tell me soon—I can't wait to apply it, whatever it is."

"I'm so grateful that you're teaching me this. I want to get my family and children (and eventual grandchildren) out of the middle class squeeze. I want them to learn how to live with money the non-debt way. Tell me more."

"Thank you for mentoring us on this. We don't know what you're going to tell us about the Fourth S, but whatever you tell us, we're going to follow your counsel. We want out of the cycle of debt, interest, and trying to make the Crank go faster and faster. We'll do what you tell us…"

A Challenge!

Do yourself a favor. Right now. Decide that *no matter what*, you're going to choose to be a Type G person as you read and apply the next chapter. This is the vitally important choice we mentioned earlier. If you make it, and do it, your finances are likely in for a major positive upgrade. Right away. And it can change the rest of your life!

Don't sit back in Type F (Fixed mindset) and make excuses. If you do, your finances probably won't improve very much. In fact, as the economy goes up and down over time, your finances will likely only get worse. And that's bad—for you and all your loved ones.

Choose right now to be a Type G person.

When you've made this decision, turn the page and read about the Fourth S of Money.

"Success is taking action towards your personal goals each day."
—*Jim Rohn*

THE FOURTH "S" OF MONEY

SOLUTION

*"I learned from everybody around me. When I was a waiter
I learned from the busboy how to quickly clear tables. I paid
attention to the businessmen's lunch conversations. I've always
been a scavenger for education. The world is full of education
if you choose to open your eyes and ears to it."*
—Robert Herjavec, Multimillionaire[52]

*"It's the men who are on missions of service, not the ones
focused on making money, who become the most successful."*
—Lauren Zander[53]

*"Rich men use most of their money to get richer.
Poor men use most of their money to look richer."*
—Mokokama Mokhonoana

The True Moneyview

Let's get right to the point. Your Crank (job, career, business, etc.) brings you income, but not just to spend. You'll spend some of it on the things you need and want, of course. But you should only spend a portion of it. Your money comes to you for a number of other reasons, and some of them are a lot more important than your expenses.

If you use your income on the most important things first, and only use what's left over on your expenses, you can see your finances and your life, happiness, relationships and successes thrive, grow and flourish. Without this understanding, many people never experience financial success.

This is the Solution: adopt a new, correct, view of money, one in which only part of your income is for (and goes to) expenses—and the rest goes to certain very special places. And apply this view of money from now on. This is the path of financial fitness.

Solution: Part I

The Solution to money challenges and a wrong view of money begins by learning about money. There is probably no way to skip this step and still obtain the results you want. Learning about money and finances is essential. As bestselling author Chris Brady put it: "Get educated about money. Get a financial education." Those who do this will be able to use their money for the right things. Those who don't could remain stuck in an incorrect view of money for a long time. And that incorrect view leads to incorrect thinking, which leads to incorrect actions, which in turn produce incorrect results.

> **It is very important to start tracking your money.**

Reading this book and really understanding the principles it teaches is an excellent start to learning about money. And later we'll recommend some additional readings, audios and other resources that will help you keep learning about money after you have completed this book.

Along with learning about money, it is very important to start tracking your money. This is very easy. Just write down everything you spend. Simply knowing this will give you a lot of increased power over your finances.

In fact, there is an even easier way to track your money—right on your smartphone. Download the Tracking App at financialfitnessinfo.com and it will help you keep track of everything you spend. Again, knowing what you spend is powerful.

For example, as one business leader put it: "I lost thirty pounds by keeping track of everything I ate. I got sick of playing soccer in the back yard with my son and feeling my belly jiggling. I was so out of breath, and I just plain decided to change things.

"Of course, everybody's physiology is different, and I'm not suggesting this for anyone else. But it worked for me. I started writing down everything I ate. Everything. I got on the scale every morning to see my weight, and I wrote down everything I put in my mouth.

"That's all I did. I didn't do a cleanse or take any special supplements or powder drinks. I just ate normal food, normal meals, everything the same—except I tracked it all. As a result, I naturally approached food differently, and I started eating healthier.

Almost everyone who truly tracks everything they spend starts spending smarter.

"I lost thirty pounds in five months doing this, because I was tracking my food. This kept me on track."

This pattern is backed up by research. For example, people who only get on a scale once a week gain an average of 2.4 pounds each year,[54] while those who weigh themselves five times a week or more lose 1.1 pounds a year on average.[55] Those who seldom or never weigh tend to gain even more. The power and principle of tracking is real.

Put simply: It makes a difference in how we approach the thing we track. If you do it with your finances, it will influence your spending and saving. And with the Tracking App, it couldn't be easier. Or, if you prefer, just write down everything you spend and keep it in your records.

Seriously, we recommend that you take just a little bit of time and track your money—all spending and income (husband and wife!). It will help you learn a lot about money, and about your financial choices and patterns.

And keep your tracking notes—forever. You'll be able to use them if you ever need to get back on track. For example, at some point you'll be able to compare your spending this month to your spending ten months ago, or five years. But only if you start keeping track.

All of this will help you learn and understand a lot more about money. Reading about money and tracking your own finances are incredibly valuable if you want to solve any money challenges and become financially fit.

Moreover, almost everyone who truly tracks everything they spend starts spending less. And they almost always start spending smarter (sometimes by simply skipping a frivolous expense in the moment). This one thing can make a huge difference for your finances.

As Brady put it: "If you keep track of all your expenses, you'll be blown away by how much you spend at Starbuck's or other places. You'll be shocked by how much you spend on sodas or snacks. Of course, everyone is different, so maybe you're spending will go to something else. But if you're tracking it, you'll be amazed at some of your expenses."

If you don't know what you're actually spending on, in specific detail, it's unlikely you'll change it much. But if you do know, you can easily make some significant improvements to your finances—just because you track everything you spend.

The purpose of tracking your expenses isn't to turn you into a "money grubber" or a Scrooge, but rather to help you have more power over your finances and greater awareness. You'll still get to buy what you choose to buy, but just knowing what you're spending your money on can help you improve what you want to purchase. Instead of mindless buying, you'll buy what you really want, and you'll naturally get better at managing your finances.

> **The true view of money is that it is meant to be a Stewardship, a Resource, and a Slave.**

Together, the action of tracking whatever you spend and also learning more about money—reading about the principles of financial fitness over time—will help you begin to almost effortlessly upgrade and enhance your financial choices. You'll know more about money, and about your own use of money, and this will almost always help you make better and more effective financial choices.

These two things—learning more about money and tracking your money—give you greater financial power. They are the first part of the money Solution; they are the practical first steps toward adopting a correct money view.

Solution: Part II

The next step of solving and overcoming money problems, and upgrading your finances in general, is to actually gain a true view of what money is. Most people don't know. As we discussed in Chapter 3, most people think money is something you earn and then spend on things you want—but this is the wrong moneyview. It leads to numerous financial problems for the people who believe it.

The true view of money is that it is meant to be:

- A Stewardship
- A Resource
- A Slave

It is important to understand each of these.

A Stewardship

First, your money is meant to be a Stewardship. This means that there are some very important things you should use it for. These things are closely connected with your Life Purpose.

If you know your Life Purpose, excellent. If not, it's very important to think about it. It can have a great positive influence on your finances, because knowing your Life Purpose tells you a lot about what money you need and how to use it more effectively.

At some point he realized that this was a true passion for him.

A Life Purpose is an overarching mission for your life, something you want to give back to God on this earth. It might be helping the poor or healing the sick, or it could be spreading beauty (through art, music, or in some other way) or healing dysfunctional families. It could be promoting leadership among youth or helping protect and spread freedom, helping poor Nicaraguan children get uniforms so they can attend their local school, or it could be any number of other things.

Your Life Purpose can be surprising. For example, Felix Kjellberg (gamer name "PewDiePie") struggled through school because he preferred playing video games to studying.[56] At some point he realized that this was more than merely that he liked to play more than work—it was a true passion for him.[57] So he got serious and began building a YouTube channel and a business that promoted and spread his passion. Six years later his business is thriving, with over 42 million subscribers, and he reportedly makes more than $12 million a year.[58]

Or compare Cameron Mitchell, who ran away from a difficult home situation at age 16 and tried to live on the streets.[59] He soon returned home, promising his mother he'd shape up. One day, after getting a job washing dishes at a local restaurant in Columbus, Ohio, he realized how much he liked working in the food industry. "I loved the pandemonium," he said. "Clear as a bell, I knew the restaurant business was where I wanted to be the rest of my life."[60]

Since that time, he has been working to build his dream. "Now, as CEO of Cameron Mitchell Restaurants, he runs 48 upscale eateries like Hudson 29 and Ocean Prime in 18 cities, with more than $250 million in annual revenue."[61] He said: "Once I fell in love with the restaurant business, you couldn't outwork me."[62]

Of course, your Life Purpose may not be a video game or restaurant business, but whatever it is, it will build on your passion and can be a motivation and focus of your work. Your Life Purpose may bring you financial profits through business success, like the two examples above, or you may work in another job or career and use money from your efforts to support your Life Purpose.

But how does one know his or her Life Purpose? A few powerful questions can help. For example, really ponder the answers to each of the following:

- What would you do with your time if you had all the time and money you could ever use—if you never had to work for money, but could just do what you really want to do that would improve the world?
- What really makes your life tick?
- What would you do if you weren't afraid?
- What would you do if you knew your efforts could change or greatly improve one thing in the world? Or in your community, town, or a group you love?

"Clear as a bell, I knew… where I wanted to be for the rest of my life."

These are good questions to help clarify your Life Purpose. What is the thing you want to do most in your life—beyond your own needs and hobbies? How would you spend your life serving

God if you had the time and resources to do whatever feels right to you? What is your deepest passion?

Your Life Purpose is extremely important to your finances, because your finances are meant to help you achieve and fulfill your Life Purpose. That's why money is a stewardship, because you earn it to help build and accomplish your Life Purpose.

> **Your Life Purpose is extremely important to your finances, because your finances are meant to help you achieve and fulfill your Life Purpose.**

This is an important mental shift. It is vital to know the difference between a life of earning money to spend on the things you need and want versus a life of earning money to build your Life Purpose. Of course, you'll pay for your needs and your family's needs as part of life—but the Life Purpose is meant to be dominant.

With this understanding, money takes on a whole new dimension. For example, if your Life Purpose is helping villages in Africa get better water sources, you're going to need more money than just paying for your family's home, clothing, food and other necessities. If your Life Purpose is spreading the principles of leadership to people who are caught in an employment rut and don't yet realize that they can be real leaders, you are going to want some extra money to help achieve this.

That's what your stewardship is. You aren't earning money just to buy stuff, you're earning it to take care of your family and to fulfill your Life Purpose. And this is incredibly important—to your finances, and also to your sense of fulfillment and happiness in life.

Your Life Purpose influences how much money you're going to need, how well you take care of it, and what you do with it. If your Life Purpose is helping inner city youth go camping and learn better life skills, you'll need to afford transportation, meals, camping gear, leaders, counselors, speakers, marketing, insurance, etc. Every Life Purpose needs a level of funding.

If this is your mindset about money, you'll approach it differently than if you just want to pay the bills and go to a movie or dinner this weekend. You'll know that you have a stewardship, and that your money has the purpose of helping your stewardship.

With this different moneyview, you'll approach your life differently—because your stewardship is different. It's not *your* money to blow. It's money for your stewardship. You'll take care of it as stewardship. If you need more of it—even a lot more—you'll put your mind to figuring out how to fund it.

This changes your entire mindset and moneyview, and therefore your actions regarding money. To repeat: money is a stewardship, meant to help you accomplish your Life Purpose. When you realize this, when you switch your thinking to this approach, you'll almost always start on the path to better financial fitness and success.

A Resource

Now, with your new, more correct view of money as a stewardship, you are ready to use money for its real purpose. Your new view is now that money is a resource. In fact, it is helpful to rank this resource right up there with oxygen!

Think about it: If you were on the moon or somewhere else without free oxygen, you wouldn't let your last tank of oxygen go to waste, right? You probably wouldn't spend your last tank of oxygen for almost anything, truth be told. But how often do we hear someone say something like "I spent my last dime to get a Corvette!"

> **"I spent my last little bit of oxygen to buy a Corvette." Not likely.**

We wouldn't do that with our last few breaths of oxygen! Imagine it: "I spent my last little bit of oxygen to buy a Corvette." Not likely.

Money is a resource just like oxygen or water. If you understand that just exchanging it for things you want to buy is a much lower priority than your family's needs and your Life Purpose, you'll treat it differently. Specifically, your money is to be used for two main things:

- Personal and family needs/wants
- Achieving your Life Purpose

If you don't have enough money to effectively fund both of these, you probably need to make a change. It is crucial to accomplish both of these things, and money is a vital resource is making them happen. Again, if you need more money to truly do them both, you'll need to figure out how to bring in more money.

> **Money is a resource for meeting the needs of your family and building your Life Mission.**

Or, if you need to change your spending or saving habits to do both of these vitally important goals, you'll realize how important such changes are. Knowing about both of these objectives (cover your family needs and accomplish your Life Mission) helps you clarify just how much money you need and how you'll use it. It helps you see money for what it really, truly, is: a resource to help you do these two things, and do them well!

Since most people have long been taught an incorrect view of money, this correct view bears repeating: Money is a resource for meeting the needs of your family and building your Life Mission. Getting this moneyview correct is essential. It is the foundation of effective money decisions, and the beginning of financial fitness.

A Slave

In addition to being a stewardship and a resource, your money is also supposed to be your slave. Specifically, this means that your money is supposed to work for *you*—rather than you always working for *it*.

How does this work? The key to making your money a slave is to build assets. Assets include anything that pays you money each month, year, etc. In other words, anything that generates positive cash flow. Most people don't have a lot of assets beyond their job, and a job is a high-maintenance asset because it requires you to keep going to work in order to collect a paycheck.

> Einstein said that compound interest is the eighth wonder of the world, but someone should have added that assets are the ninth!

Low maintenance assets are the best in the long term, because they keep paying you even when you don't go to work. For example, an interest-bearing savings account pays you interest even if you don't show up at your job for a while. (Okay, we admit, really, really *low* amounts of interest!)

Thus the money in your savings account is your slave: it pays you over and over. *It* does the work—so you don't have to. Many investments can do the same thing. And ownership of a business can pay you over and over as well—you receive money from the profits of the business, not just from a paycheck.

But what exactly is an asset? The answer is very important. You know something is an asset if the dollar you put somewhere pays you back—over and over. For example, when you put money in an interest-bearing savings account, and leave it there, it pays you a bit of money back year after year.

> **You know something is an asset if the dollar you put somewhere pays you back—over and over.**

If the dollar doesn't pay you back repeatedly, it's an expense or a liability, or a non-asset savings. If it's an expense, do your best not to pay interest on it—live as much as possible without debt. If it's a liability, minimize it—have as few liabilities as possible. If it's a non-asset savings, like money under your mattress, at least it's not costing you. And you might need it in a time of emergency or natural disaster.

But put most of your savings, and a lot of your effort, into building assets. The goal is to increase your assets over time, continuously. That's how you make money your slave.

In fact, as much as possible, make it automatic. Every time you make a deposit, have the bank send 10 percent or more of the deposit to your long-term savings account (or other investments). This builds assets consistently.

Any asset that pays you repeatedly, even if you don't show up to earn it, is a low maintenance asset. The money you put into such assets is your slave—it just keeps on working for you, even after you've stopped working for it.

You want to put as much money as you can to work for you (as assets), so you have to work less and less for it. This is profound. Einstein said that compound interest is the eighth wonder of the world, but someone should have added that assets may be the ninth!

Assets are really powerful. As you consistently use part of the money you earn from your job, career or business to build assets, the assets can eventually (and increasingly) create a situation where you have to work less and less—because you're getting more and more money from them.

This is the opposite of the "work 'til you die plan." Building assets allows you to eventually roll around on the carpet with your grandkids, instead of hurry off to work. Or, if you start early enough, roll around on the carpet with your kids a lot more than you would otherwise have time to do.

Again, most people have a wrong view of money because they think they are supposed to earn most of it from their work. The truth is that you should earn most of your money in the long run from your assets.

> **Again, most people have a wrong view of money because they think they are supposed to earn most of it from their work.**

This bears repeating—and repeating and repeating, until we really get it. Part of the money you earn from your job is always supposed to be used to help you build up assets. As long as you are working, you need to be putting some of your paycheck into assets—particularly low maintenance assets that will keep paying you, whether you go to work or not.

With this approach, the older you get, the less and less you have to chase the dollar, and the more you let the dollar (from your assets) take care of you. This is the one major thing that sets "haves" apart from the "have nots."

In short: money should be your slave, and you should use it as mentioned above not just to pay your bills or buy stuff but to truly accomplish your Life Purpose. This is the correct view of money, and having/following the correct view of money is the Solution to money challenges. It is the Solution to financial flabbiness and can help you become a lot more financially successful.

Solution: Part III

The third part of the money Solution is to get out of debt. In fact, if you have a lot of debt, or even a little, pay as much as you can to it (10 percent or more) each time you get paid. This one choice, to always put some of your paycheck toward your debt, can make a huge positive difference in your finances. After all, how difficult is it going to be to build positive cash flowing assets when you are paying money toward interest on loans for consumerism instead? Answer: Almost impossible.

We recommend that you start by paying off your highest interest credit card first, and then, once it is paid off, add the amount you normally paid to it to overpay on the next card. This allows you to pay off the next card at even more rapid pace, and you repeat with the third card. This "snowballing" technique is very effective.

Of course, keep paying the minimum balances on all your cards while you do this so that you won't incur extra fees or run into other problems. If you want more help on this, including a program that walks you through the details of getting out of debt using the "snowball" and "debt rolldown" technique and other tools, get the *Financial Fitness Workbook* from financialfitnessinfo.com.

The truth is that you should earn most of your money in the long run from your assets.

One of the main challenges in getting out of debt is that many people have a serious debt habit. Some of them—as debt addicts—will likely tell you that paying off debts and building up savings isn't easy, that it's actually extremely hard. And they might even add that you don't need to bother—just keep getting more debt to pay the old debt, and buy even more stuff.

Don't listen to financial advice from people who are broke and/or addicted to debt.

But that's all a myth. Don't listen to financial advice from people who are broke and/or addicted to debt. The truth is that getting out of debt is literally as simple as choosing to pay a specific percentage of every paycheck to your highest interest credit card or other debt—and then just doing it. Over and over, consistently, until all your debt is gone. It can take a long time, if your debt is substantial, but it isn't complex.

Those who do this, even though it may sometimes *feel* difficult, can eventually get out of debt and on the path of financial growth. Those who don't do this nearly always keep experiencing money

Struggles. Again, the *Financial Fitness Workbook* is specifically geared to help people get out of debt—if you need it, this can be a very helpful resource.

Conclusion

As long as you have the wrong view of the Crank and what it's for, you'll likely face financial Struggles. Relying only on the Crank (job, career, etc.) is how our nation got to the place outlined in the above chapter on Statistics, with high debt, difficulty making ends meet, a declining standard of living for most people, and a serious middle class squeeze.

Building assets is the powerful Solution and key to lifting your finances to a whole new, more prosperous level—a level that can help you more effectively meet your family's needs/wants and also more successfully and aggressively obtain the resources necessary to fully achieve your Life Purpose.

"He is invited to great things who receives small things greatly."
—*Flavius*

THE FIFTH "S" OF MONEY
Strategy

"We are engineered mentally to move progressively and successively from one goal to the next, and we are never really happy unless, and until, we are moving toward the accomplishment of something that is important to us."
—Brian Tracy

"Concerning investments, you have to get educated. Don't rely on some expert, and don't be intimidated by fancy financial terms, titles, or tall glass buildings. Get the investment education for yourself so you really know what you're doing."
—Chris Brady

"If you want to know the secret of [investing], read Aesop's tale of the tortoise and the hare."
—Former President of a Fortune 500 Company[63]

Refocus the Crank

The way to get your money working for you is really very simple. Refocus the Crank. It's what happens downstream of the Crank that matters.

In other words, instead of using the Crank (your job, career, work) to get money that you spend on your needs and wants, put the first part of all money you receive from the Crank to savings. Pay yourself first.

Pay your future and your Life Mission first. In short: put the first fruits of all money you make to building assets. We recommend that adults put a minimum of 20 percent of every dollar you earn to building assets (youth should put at least 50 percent).

> **It's what happens downstream of the Crank that matters.**

Here's how this works. Each time you get paid or receive money, give 10 percent to tithing and then at least 20 to savings. More specifically:

- 10% to tithing
- 10% to an emergency fund
- 10% to long-term savings asset development

First Step: Giving

Start right now by giving the first 10 percent of every paycheck you receive to a worthy cause or causes. No matter how broke you are, give some of your money to tithing and to help people. Giving makes your heart right. It's the right thing to do. This is so important. This is a foundation of financial fitness.

Second Step: Emergency Fund

Open a separate checking account for this, and build up an emergency fund to at least $1,000 as quickly as you can, by putting at least 10 percent of all money you receive in it. This will give you greater financial peace of mind and real resources when a "rainy day" comes along—such as broken water pipes in the basement, a car that needs new tires, etc.

Once you have $1,000 in your emergency account, build it to $5,000. The objective is to put away 3-6 months of living expenses to this account. And if you ever spend some of it on an emergency, replenish it as quickly as possible.

When you have your 6 months of expenses set aside in your emergency fund, you can stop paying into it and put that 10 percent (or higher, if possible) toward paying off your debts even faster, or to your long-term asset development.

Third Step: Long Term Savings (Asset Development)

As you build up your long-term savings, you'll be building and growing an asset that will be a great blessing for your family, your service to others, and your Life Purpose. Put this money in a secure, FDIC insured (or equivalent in your nation**), bank savings account, and keep it growing every time you get paid.

As you replace your income from the Crank with income from your assets, you'll become more and more financially fit.

**You may even want to investigate internet only banks, as they seem to be paying the highest rates of passbook/checking account interest these days.

Later, when you have a lot of money in this account, you'll be able to transfer some of it to other investments. (More on this below.) But you never want to spend this money. Always keep it growing—either in a regular savings account or in one of the other kinds of investments we'll talk about below.

The key is that this savings keeps paying you money each year in the form of interest or investment profits. The interest or profit is the money you can spend, because it didn't come from the Crank, it comes from your assets.

The more assets you build, and the greater their value, the more you'll be paid by assets rather than directly for your job or work. As you replace your income from the Crank with income from your assets, you'll become more and more financially fit. Eventually, if you build enough assets, you can make enough from your assets to retire from the Crank, if you want to, and give your full attention to your family and your Life Purpose.

Or you may decide to keep your job and use the extra money for more assets or to grow your Life Mission even more. Whatever you decide to do at that point, you'll be able to focus on what you really want because you'll have the assets to pay for your life, family needs/wants, and Life Purpose.

Fourth Step: The YOU, Inc. Investment Hierarchy

The next step of your financial fitness Strategy is to begin using some of your savings to invest. Here is the You, Inc. Investment Hierarchy, as developed by Chris Brady and Orrin Woodward:

Work on this plan from the bottom up, starting with Level 1. Note that the investments generally get riskier the higher up the hierarchy you go. At first, the overall Strategy is to minimize your involvement in Levels 6-7 while maximizing Levels 1-4. The reason for this is that Levels 6-7 require expertise that will take you some time to acquire.

In other words, if stocks, bonds or real estate are your primary business, then you'll likely gain the mastery to invest wisely and effectively in the field of your career. If not, tread carefully. A lot of people lose their hard-won savings by speculating in fields they haven't truly mastered (in essence, by jumping up the hierarchy too soon before first securing each of the levels below).

Let's learn more about each Level of the You, Inc. Investment Hierarchy.

Level 1: Invest in Yourself

This is the most basic and foundational part of investing, and as such it is probably the most important. In fact, that's why we name it the You, Inc. Investment Hierarchy. This is you treating yourself like a business. You're the company. Making you better,

> *You* **are the best investment you could ever make!**

making you great, is your main focus. That's what investing in yourself is all about.

You are the best investment you could ever make! *You* are your best asset.

Specifically, there are at least three main parts of effectively investing in yourself. First, learn as much as you can about money and finances. Become a voracious reader and student of everything financial.

Of course, don't learn about money and finances from people who are broke! This will just teach you the wrong lessons, and you probably won't like the results. But *do* read and learn from those who have built up the kind of assets you want to have and who live the kind of lifestyle you want to live. Also, learn from those who are using their money well—to accomplish their Life Purposes.

Searching out books, audios and materials on finances from such people and learning all you can from them is a great part of investing in yourself. Here are some specific materials we recommend for your further study of financial fitness:

- *Financial Fitness: The Offense, Defense, and Playing Field of Personal Finance,* Foreword by Chris Brady and Orrin Woodward
- *Financial Fitness for Teens,* Foreword by Chris Brady
- *Financial Fitness Pack,* with book and audios
- *Financial Fitness Workbook*
- Financial Master Class, audio and video workshop

- *The Financial Matrix,* by Orrin Woodward
- *Paradigm Shift: 7 Realities of Success in the New Economy,* Foreword by George Guzzardo
- *The Tools of Money: Hands-On Financial Skills for Teens, Parents, and Adults*

A second part of investing in yourself is to become a voracious reader in general. Knowledge is power, as the old saying goes. The more you learn and know, the more intellectual resources you'll have for your work, finances, and even your Life Mission.

Learn about finances from those who have built up the kind of assets you want to have and who live the kind of lifestyle you want to live.

Read widely, and read deeply. Read history, literature, biographies, self-help and leadership materials, and anything that will help you improve yourself. "Leaders are readers," as Harry Truman put it.

A third key to investing in yourself is to consider starting your own business. There are many financial benefits to business ownership, both for those who work full time on their own business and also for people who build a part-time, evening, weekend or even hobby business. There are tax benefits and significant potential income opportunities to building your own business—even a small one.

Moreover, the greatest benefit to business ownership for many people is what they learn about leadership, finances, their own strengths and weaknesses, how to work with people and build great relationships, etc. Building a business can be a very effective way to invest in yourself and learn a great deal.

Likewise, when you build your own business you can invest directly in it and you'll likely have a bigger-than-usual level of control over the success of your investment. When you invest in what you really know, and what you are really good at, you can almost always achieve much higher returns than when you have little control over the organizations you invest in. This approach is clearly outlined in the book *The Warren Buffett Way*. As one report put it it: "Warren Buffett...believes in tilting the scales as far as possible away from speculation, and toward an owner-ship-minded investing framework."[64]

In summary, the first and most foundational level of investing is to invest in yourself: your financial knowledge, your overall leadership and life education, and, if you choose, your own business. Investing in yourself brings great educational and personal returns because as *you* improve, your life generally improves. And your ability to further improve your life increases as well.

Level 2: Survival Savings

The second level is very important, but many people overlook it—and some people take it to the extreme. Without getting carried away, it is wise to realize that things happen in the course of human events. It is smart to put away some cash savings in a safe and hidden place in your home or in a bank vault, along with some silver (for easy exchange in times of natural disaster or other emergency) and gold (for storing value).

Also put away some food storage, water storage (especially necessary in many natural disasters), batteries, and other things you might need. Perhaps store some ammunition and a hunting rifle, or some antibiotics in case none are available. The money you put into these things will be well spent if you ever need them.

Overall, give some thought to what you might need in the case of a serious emergency in your area, and wisely plan and prepare ahead. You may never need it, but you'll never resent being prepared for an emergency.

This level is very basic. But floods, tornadoes, hurricanes and other emergencies do happen, and a little preparation goes a long way if you ever experience such calamities.

It's also important to put away some savings in gold and silver, to store your value if a national or international financial emergency ever comes. If the government ever declares that our dollars or other currency aren't worth anything anymore, or even just change the value of what they're worth by law, gold and silver has its own value and will likely be the only type of money that retains its value.

Gold and silver aren't really about investment, since metal values don't really go up or down much (outside of price swings due to either currency debasement or speculative purchases). In fact, gold and silver have remained quite stable for a very long time. It is the price of dollars, pounds, yen and other currency that have fluctuated around the price of gold and silver, not vice versa.

For example, if you went back to 1900 and called the value of a dollar at that time exactly one dollar, the value of that dollar today is 4 cents. This means that 96 percent of the purchasing power of a dollar has been lost since that time. In contrast, gold and silver have held their value.

Again, keeping gold and silver is about storing value. It's a lot like "freezing the fruit." For example, you pick strawberries in the summer, and wish you could have fresh strawberry pie in the dead of winter. Well, by freezing a bag of strawberries you allow yourself to pull them out long after the strawberry plants are frozen—and make yourself and others a nice dessert.

Financially fit people have learned to "freeze the fruit" of their labor by storing some of it in gold and silver. If government currency ever crashes, those with gold and silver will still have a savings.

Level 3: Emergency Fund

This level is the same emergency fund discussed in the Third Step above. To reiterate: Open a separate checking account and put at least 10 percent of everything you earn into this fund, every time you get paid. Build it up to at least $1,000 and then ultimately 3-6 months of your regular living expenses. This fund will put you on a whole new level of financial fitness.

Level 4: Savings, Long Term and Targeted

This level is a very, very important part of your financial fitness. People who don't build a long-term savings account, and keep adding to it over time, seldom become financially fit.

As we mentioned above, always put at least 10 percent of your paycheck and other income into a long-term savings account. And never spend it. Keep building and growing your long-term savings for the rest of your life. This one thing can greatly increase your financial fitness.

> Always put at least 10 percent of your paycheck and other income into a long-term savings account.

Put this money in a secure interest-bearing bank account, as mentioned earlier, and keep it growing—with each and every paycheck. You'll be excited over time to see it expand and multiply.

Other savings that are part of Level 4 and can help you build assets are a 401(k) (or equivalent in other nations), a Roth IRA, whole term life insurance, and some annuities. Be sure to research any savings program before you put money into it, and make sure it is secure and also an asset that will pay you back plus extra over time.

Another important kind of savings in Level 4 is Targeted Savings. This helps you buy "that thing you just gotta have!" For example, if you ever think there is some product or service and you'll "just die without it!," use targeted savings. Instead of buying the item with debt, put a specific percentage of every paycheck into savings and keep saving until you can buy the item with cash. This is how financially fit people get those special things they feel they'll: "just die if I don't have it!"

> "There's something I really want to buy, but I'm not going to use a penny of debt or pay 1 single cent of interest. I'm going to save up until I can buy it outright with cash."

On a humorous note, another option is to not buy it for a week and then see if you're dead. Chances are you'll still be alive, and you'll know that you aren't going to die without it. But if you really want it, and can't let it go, saving for it in a targeted savings account is the smart way to go.

This keeps you out of debt, and you'll pay a lot less for the item because you won't pay any interest. In fact, you can combine saving up for it in a targeted savings with also buying it during a sale. Waiting for the store to put it on a special sale can be really smart.

But don't do the opposite and use debt because you want to get it while it's still on sale! That's just justification of unwise spending. Don't get sucked into marketing schemes either, such as "no cash down," "0% financing," "90 days same as cash," "no payments for 12 months," etc. It's all still debt.

Whatever the item is that you feel you simply must have, don't use debt. Build up your targeted savings. This is usually best done by opening a separate savings account and keeping your targeted money in one place.

In short, targeted savings means: "There's something I really want to buy, and I'm going to buy it, but I'm not going to use a penny of debt or pay 1 single cent of interest—I'm going to save up until I can buy it outright with cash. And even then I'll look for a sale or coupon, if possible."

Level 5: CDs, Money Market Accounts, Bonds

At some point, if you follow the Strategy and steps outlined in this chapter, you'll have enough stored in your long-term savings account that it will be wise to put some of it into other investments—because they pay higher interest rates and/or higher returns. In essence, it will be time to move up the hierarchy.

Some of these investments are quite "secure", meaning that the risk of losing your money in them is low. These are the Level 5 investments, and include CDs, money market accounts, and the safer types of bonds.

A lot of investment books, workshops and advisors downplay these investments because they have relatively low returns (compared to some stocks, some real estate, etc.). But these low returns also come with low risk. Level 5 is all about getting a little more return than a regular savings account, but not investing in anything risky.

As you put some money into such investments, be sure to know the details. With CDs, for instance, whatever money you put in will be tied up for a pre-determined amount of time. So if you're going to want it later, you should leave it in a regular savings account or another place where it is more liquid (easily accessible).

There are a number of other details that you'll need to know about any place you put your savings beyond a regular savings account. Do your homework on any such investments or accounts. Don't transfer your savings until you understand the details.

Level 6: Stocks and Real Estate

This level of investing is more risky than the first five. In fact, it can be very risky. While many books and materials on investing recommend these Level 6 type investments due to examples of high returns, we take a different approach.

The rule of thumb is to invest in what you know.

The rule of thumb is to invest in what you know. In other words, avoid investing in anything—any field or business sector or specific business—that you don't really know a lot about. If you're not an expert on it, don't invest in it. Likewise, don't invest any of your long-term savings in Levels 6 or 7.

As mentioned above, this approach is sometimes known as "The Warren Buffet Way," from the bestselling book by this same title. And as one report summarized:

> "...the whole idea of 'investing in what you know' was first popularized by Peter Lynch, one of the most successful investors in history. In his 13 years managing the Fidelity Magellan fund...Lynch wracked up annual returns that averaged 29%—such an absurdly high number that investment calculators won't even let you plug it in.... Wall Street, of course, prefers that you follow a much more complicated investment scheme that will generate higher fees."[65]

Again, the financially fit path is to only invest money that you can afford to lose in any field or business that you haven't mastered. Some people do make a lot of money in stocks or real estate investing, but many of those people are full time stock or real estate investors. Most of them know what they are doing—deeply, with long experience. And most of them have had their share of losses as well. If you aren't a professional stock or real estate investor, be very careful with such investments.

If you can't afford to lose the money, keep it in Levels 1-5. Be careful investing in Levels 6-7. However, there are some smart ways to navigate these waters. Index Mutual Funds (with low fees and no "churn"), and Exchange Traded Funds (ETFs) that also follow market indexes, can be a very smart choice for the individual investor. These two vehicles are available for both bonds and stocks, and are often even part of the choices in 401(k)'s IRA's, and other tax-advantaged accounts. Again, become well informed about these vehicles before diving in.

Level 7: Speculative Ventures, Start-Ups, Inventions

This level will come to you naturally as you build up your savings and assets. When people realize that you have money, some of them will want to offer various "investment opportunities" to you. Maybe a lot of them!

Many people have lost money by agreeing to invest this way with friends, family members and others who are close to them. At times this causes serious relationship issues as well. Be wise when dealing with such investments—

If you can't afford to lose the money, keep your investments in Levels 1-5.

with people you know, and with anyone else as well.

Specifically, don't invest in Level 7 any money that you can't afford to lose. And if you do invest, only invest a little.

The overall rule remains the same at Level 7 as on all the other levels: avoid investing in anything outside your areas of personal mastery. Most importantly, don't ever invest in a situation where you are liable for what happens but aren't closely involved in the decision-making or don't have control over the management.

The little things—like getting out of debt, paying yourself first, and focusing on the first 4 Levels of the Investment Hierarchy—can make all the difference in how you deal with money.

Conclusion

The very best investment Strategy is to focus on Levels 1-4, and when you've built up enough resources, then carefully in Level 5 and higher. Again, avoid investing in things outside your personal expertise.

"Be ashamed to die until you have won some victory for humanity."
—Horace Mann

CONCLUSION

Do Try This At Home!

*"The last play is history,
the next play is everything."*
—Hugh O'Neill

*"The holidays can be a really good time to buy
gold and silver because lots of people trade in
precious metals to buy plastic toys!"*
—Chris Brady

"As ye sow, so shall ye reap."
—Galatians 6:7

The Crux

As you earn money in your life, put some of it (at least 10 percent) into building assets—each and every time you get paid. This is the opposite of what most people do, and it is largely the difference between those who are broke and in debt versus those who are financially fit.

The truth is that people who consistently build assets over time, spend wisely and frugally, and focus on accomplishing their Life Purpose, usually do better financially than a lot of people who are smarter, have more prestigious credentials or job titles, were born to a family with money, or enjoy other natural advantages.

> **Pretty much everyone has to work for their money (the Crank), but most people *only* work for their money.**

The long term, consistent saving of resources, wise spending, and building of assets is a powerful and effective path to financial fitness. People who don't follow it—whatever their background or past experience—seldom do well with money.

As we discussed, assets bring more money to you, more cashflow, often regardless of what you do. Pretty much everyone has to work for their money (the Crank), but most people *only* work for their money. They work and spend, and keep on working and spending. The financially fit, in contrast, consistently convert a piece of every paycheck into assets.

They put a portion of all their income in savings and other interest- and profit-paying financial vehicles that consistently pay them more money over time. This nearly always moves them from a life of money Struggles to one of financial fitness.

Two Kinds of People...

Indeed, financially speaking, to paraphrase an old proverb: "There are two kinds of people in the world: Those who have assets, and those who don't." The truth is that most people don't have enough assets to live on the interest or dividends. Thus, they are the people "who don't." They are the "have nots" in our world.

The people "who do" have assets are relatively few in society, but they are financially fit. And there are actually a lot of them.[66] Such financial fitness is frequently the simple result of putting a percentage of their money each time they get paid into the four items discussed in this book:

> "There are two kinds of people in the world: Those who have assets, and those who don't."

1. Giving (at least 10 percent)
2. Long-Term Savings (at least 10 percent)
3. Emergency Fund (wisely)
4. The You, Inc. Investment Hierarchy (wisely and progressively)

Those who build all four of these things, every time they get paid, naturally grow their assets, resources, and reservoirs. Most of them also use part of these resources to accomplish important Life Purposes that greatly bless the world.

In fact, if you know your Life Purpose, and you know just how crucial it is to consistently build these four items—following the four will have a great impact on how effectively you can spread your Life Purpose to serve God, bless others, and improve the world in your unique way.

> "Don't ever think that following the right money principles means you have to live a miserly, sad life. It doesn't."

Two Diverging Roads

In all this talk about money, perhaps the most ironic thing is that people who follow the Crank Path (work for all your money, buy stuff using debt, and then work harder as your debt grows) often don't have as many nice things as those who use the Asset Path (work hard and put a piece of every paycheck in long-term savings, practice delayed gratification, focus on building assets, and grow assets to help accomplish your Life Purpose). Despite the myth that using debt will help you get the nice things you want in life, it actually tends to work out the opposite.

As one business leader put it: "The weird thing is, when I talk to people who are totally in debt—say $279,000 in debt between their mortgage and credit cards, for example—I often look around, and their house isn't that nice, their stuff isn't that good. Where did the money go?

"In contrast, I talk to people who are debt free, who put most of their money into assets until they were making enough from assets to buy what they want, and they have really nice stuff. It's the weirdest thing. It's hard to describe, but when they got on the right path, the Asset Path, they ended up with the good stuff."

As Chris Brady said: "Don't ever think that following the right money principles means you have to live a miserly, sad life. It doesn't. Building the right financial habits, the habits of wise spending and growing assets, starts to really multiply over time. It's the people who use the job, debt and Crank approach who are always struggling with their finances."

When you build assets over time, you don't have to deal with the overextended expenses, debt, and other forces that have created a nation of Statistics like those we learned about in the first chapter. Instead, you put a lot more of the money you earn into assets, and over time the assets become your slave and pay you enough to live the life you really desire and have the kind of stuff you really want.

These two paths couldn't be much more opposite. Yet for some reason most people choose the lesser one.

That's not really so surprising when you think about it, because the Asset Path is a radical shift away from how most of us were raised. The large majority of people were trained in the Crank Path, pure and simple.

To review, the right path—the Asset Path, the road of financial fitness—includes the following overall Strategy:

1. Pay yourself first (in the types of savings listed above, such as investing in yourself and your own business, survival savings, emergency fund, long-term savings).

2. Automate it (make it as automatic as possible, so the transfers to savings happen every time you get paid without you having to do anything).

3. Work from the bottom of the You, Inc. Investment Hierarchy towards the top, focusing on Levels 1-4, and being very careful about Levels 5-7.

4. As your assets grow, and when you have the resources, spread them out so if some of them go down others will still be there—some in cash in a safe place, some in savings, some in precious metals, some in bonds, and maybe some in whole life insurance, annuities, etc. (Of course, really educate yourself on the various kinds of assets so you can make wise decisions.)

This is an effective road to assets, and a path to financial fitness and financial freedom. It is also a road to greater resources for your Life Purpose.

> You only have to get good at this once, and then stick with it. It will bless your entire life.

Perhaps the most amazing thing about it all is just how simple it is. Just look at the 4 very basic items above. Do them, and financial fitness increases.

In short, you can do this—starting right now. It's so simple. And the results are exciting and effective. They can change everything for your finances. You just have to do the first 3 simple things, and keep doing them. Then, as you have more assets and money and learn more about different kinds of assets, you can add in item 4.

But the first 3 will get you to a whole new level of financial fitness, if you consistently apply them. As you do, your financial future can be incredibly bright. Financial stress can leave your chest and be out of your life. You can breathe in financial improvement as you apply correct principles that truly work.

Perhaps the best news of all: You only have to get good at this once, and then stick with it. It will bless your entire life. And you can teach it to your children and posterity.

> Financial fitness doesn't have to be complicated or hard. These baby steps are simple and easy.

These baby steps are simple and easy. Financial fitness doesn't have to be complicated or hard. It really isn't. As you implement these 3 simple items (always pay yourself first, automate it, and work from the bottom of the You, Inc. Investment Hierarchy up) you can watch your finances improve, grow and flourish.

This can make such a major positive difference in your financial future—for your whole family and for generations to come. The 5 S's of money clearly support and reinforce the reality that financially fit people have known for centuries: the Asset Path is the correct road to financial fitness. And guess what? Anybody can get on and stay on this Path.

NOTES

1. Center for American Progress.

2. "The Middle Class in America has just become a minority," Mybudget360.com.

3. See ibid.

4. Center for American Progress.

5. *Esquire*, February 2016, 56.

6. Ibid.

7. Todd Campbell, "The Average American Has This Much Debt…" *The Motley Fool*, January 18, 2015.

8. ValuePenguin.com, "Average Credit Card Debt in America: 2016 Facts and Figures"

9. "Welcome to the new model of retirement. No retirement." Mybudget360.com.

10. "The New Pace of Retirement," Raymond James ad, 2015.

11. Fareed Zakaria, "Can America Be Fixed?" *Foreign Affairs*, January/February 2013, 26.

12. Ibid.

13. Harry S. Dent, 2015, *The Demographic Cliff*, New York: Penguin, 119, 303.

14. Ibid.

15. Anthony B. Atkinson, "How to Spread the Wealth," *Foreign Affairs*, January/February 2016, 29.

16. Ronald Inglehart, "Inequality and Modernization," *Foreign Affairs*, January/February 2016, 2.

17. Ibid. Statistics are from 2011.

18. *Esquire*, February 2016, 57.

19. Ibid., 61.

20. Federal Reserve Bank of Minneapolis, *Quarterly Review*, July 2004.

21. BankruptcyAction.com.

22. "Why Middle Class Mothers and Fathers Are Going Broke," *Today. com*, December 12, 2003.

23. 2007 Statistics.

24. Derek Thompson, "Very Sad Graph," *TheAtlantic.com*, August 1, 2012.

25. Harry S. Dent, 2015, *The Demographic Cliff*, New York: Penguin, 101-102.

26. Ibid., 102.

27. See Matthew Desmond, *Evicted*. Cited in Crown publishing ad.

28. See ibid.

29. "The Return of the Multi-Generational Family Household," Pew Research Center, March 18, 2010.

30. Ibid.

31. Ibid.

32. Ibid.

33. "Fighting Poverty in a Bad Economy, Americans Move in With Relatives," Pew Research Center, October 3, 2011.

34. "Crisis of Generations," Mybudget360.com. See also: Pew Research Center.

35. Ibid. See also: Pew Research Center.

36. Ibid. See also: Pew Research Center.

37. Ibid.

38. "The Compression of Generations," Mybudget360.com. See also: Pew Research Center.

39. "The catastrophe of our economy for the young American worker," Mybudget360.com.

40. Ibid.

41. Boom and Bust newsletter, Harry S. Dent.

42. Ibid.

43. Ibid.

44. Neil Postman and Steve Powers, 2008, *How to Watch TV News*, New York: Penguin, 119.

45. Ibid., 125.

46. From Quickbooks and Ally Bank ads, respectively.

47. Alvin Toffler, 1981, *The Third Wave*, Bantam: New York, 59.

48. Ibid.

49. Ibid.

50. Ibid., 66.

51. Ibid.

52. Cited in Joe Kita, "The Best Money Advice I Ever Heard," *Men's Health*, March 2016.

53. Ibid.

54. Cited in *Men's Health*, March 2016, 16. Source: *Obesity*.

55. Ibid.

56. Patrick Gomez, "Making Millions…By Playing Video Games," *People*, February 22, 2016.

57. Ibid.

58. Ibid.

59. Catherine Kast, "My American Dream: Great Success Against the Odds," *People*, February 22, 2016.

60. Ibid.

61. Ibid.

62. Ibid.

63. Cited in Joe Kita, "The Best Money Advice I Ever Heard," *Men's Health*, March 2016.

64. "Invest Like a Girl (And Warren Buffett)" *U.S. News and World*

Report, Special Edition, *How to Make Money,* 2013.

65. Jack Otter, "The Biggest Fitness Fad of All," *Men's Health*, January/February 2016.

66. See the bestselling *The Millionaire Next Door* for details and statistics.

FINANCIAL FITNESS PROGRAM

Get Out of Debt and Stay Out of Debt!

FREE PERSONAL WEBSITE

SIGN UP AND TAKE ADVANTAGE OF THESE FREE FEATURES:

- Personal website
- Take your custom assessment test
- Build your own profile
- Share milestones and successes with partners and friends
- Post videos and photos
- Receive daily info "nuggets"

FINANCIAL FITNESS BASIC PROGRAM

The first program to teach all three aspects of personal finance: defense, offense, and playing field. Learn the simple, easy-to-apply principles that can help you shore up your resources, get out of debt, and build stability for a more secure future. It's all here, including a comprehensive book, companion workbook, and 8 audios that amplify the teachings from the books.

Also available DIGITALLY!

financialfitnessinfo.com

FINANCIAL FITNESS
MASTER CLASS

Buy it once and use it forever! Designed to provide a continual follow-up to the principles learned in the Basic Program, this ongoing educational support offers over 6 hours of video and over 14 hours of audio instruction that walk you through the workbook, step by step. Perfect for individual or group study.

6 videos, 15 audios

FINANCIAL FITNESS
TRACK AND SAVE

The Financial Fitness Program teaches you how to get out of debt, build additional streams of income, and properly take advantage of tax deductions. Now, with this subscription, we give you the tools to do so. The Tracker offers mobile expense tracking tools and budgeting software, while the Saver offers you thousands of coupons and discounts to help you save money every day.

THE WEALTH HABITS SERIES

The Wealth Habits series is designed to help you prosper through consistent, ongoing, simple, and enjoyable financial literacy education. You will learn timeless principles about how to better handle your money, and timely commentary on the current economic forces affecting the "playing field" upon which we all must participate. Small doses of information applied consistently over time can produce enormous results through the formation of new and profitable habits. This is what the Wealth Habits series is all about.

WEALTHABITS
SERIES

The Wealth Habits series will put you in a unique position. You will know something that only a few people in the world know. You will know the principles of financial fitness. You have the power to not only develop financial fitness but also to positively impact the lives of those around you. And the time to act is NOW.

LEARN TO NOT ONLY *SURVIVE*, BUT *THRIVE* DURING TOUGH ECONOMIC TIMES!